Praise for ⌐
A Journey to Enlightenment

"Here is a lover of God and through that a lover of humanity—the world should welcome this wonderful soul to join the great voices of Rumi and the other mystics—let us celebrate our shared humanity with Lyric and the gift of her beautiful verses." ~ **Ambassador Akbar Ahmed, Ibn Khaldun Chair of Islamic Studies at American University and Former Pakistani High Commissioner to the Uk and Ireland**

"Through Lyric Benson Fergusson's poetry, she beautifully shares glimpses of her profound spiritual journey. Her wild humor had me laughing out loud while deliciously reminding me of the divine nature of life within all of us." ~ **Marci Shimoff, #1 New York Times Bestselling Author of *Chicken Soup for the Woman's Soul* and *Happy for No Reason***

"These are startling poems—bold and unafraid—that abandon the conventional politeness we use to approach the deity. This is a pragmatic and earthy love for the creator of Earth. This is the Song of Solomon sung to a modern melody and it deserves your attention." ~ **Bill Prady, Executive Producer of CBS's *The Big Bang Theory,* ABC's *The Muppets,* and *Dharma and Greg***

"My Goodness! To read Lyric's Rumi-esque poetry is to be magically transported through the erotic thrill of a young woman's awakening in her body, mind, and soul to the unspeakable immensity of Divine Love. As her lyrical sensuality 'drags me across star fields' (her words) she masterfully unites the spiritual with the sexual—I find myself both profoundly inspired and deliciously turned on!" ~ **Bryan Reeves, Conscious Relationships Coach and Author of *The Sex, Flirting, Dating, Hunting and Hoping Diet***

"It took only fifteen minutes with Lyric Benson Fergusson's exuberant and serene new poetry to find myself wonderfully and wildly in love. With an awakened heart, Ms. Benson Fergusson sweeps us across the border of all that's familiar, into the enchantment of all that matters." ~ **Barnet Bain, Author of** *The Book of Doing and Being: Rediscovering Creativity in Life, Love and Work* **and Producer of** *What Dreams May Come* **and** *The Celestine Prophecy*

"Lyric's new collection of poems, *French Kissing God,* as its name implies, juggles sexual and sacred elements in a novel and exciting way. By turns audacious and vulnerable, this slender volume covers a broad sweep of human attributes. Though full of youthful energy and sensuality, it also signals the literary arrival of a soul both old and wise." ~ **Dr. Norman E. Rosenthal, World-Renowned Psychiatrist and New York Times Bestselling Author of** *Transcendence: Healing and Transformation Through Transcendental Meditation*

"We human beings have a great forgetfulness, and poets like Lyric Benson Fergusson are the voices that remind us again and again of our deepest longing for union with God. Through her words and images Lyric ignites again the longing that will take us home." ~ **Oriah Mountain Dreamer, Spiritual Teacher and Bestselling Author of** *The Invitation*

"This book is awesome!!! I'm totally blown away by the stunning directness of Lyric's transmission of the ONE! Her words are a flying carpet taking me, us—smoothly, swiftly, effortlessly—right into the heart of the heart of everything that matters. I thank Lyric for sharing her deep secret with such eloquence, delight, and poise—for exposing her Sacred self ... discovery ... journey... It surely will give flight, light, and sight to many a heart." ~ **Peggy O'Neill, Motivational Speaker and Author of** *Walking Tall*

"It's certainly refreshing to experience someone having a sensuous relationship with the divine. God knows we've been stuck in sanctimony and piety way too long. Lyric's courageously authentic poetry rouses the heart, tingles the soul, and wiggles the toes." ~ **Dara Marks, Hollywood's #1 Rated Script Consultant and Author of** *Inside Story: The Power of the Transformational Arc*

"Lyric reveals the true heart, that which is vulnerable and open, fiery and passionate, deep and revealing. This is mystical writing for and from the essence of soul." ~ **Simran Singh, Speaker, Visionary, and Author of** *Conversations with the Universe: How the World Speaks to Us*

"Lyric's poems express so eloquently and emotionally in a conscious form a journey we all have experienced in a state of unconscious. Albert Einstein said, 'Few are those who can see with their own eyes and feel with their own hearts.' Lyric's poetry can start you on a journey to be among those few." ~ **Billy Mills, Olympic Gold Medalist, Lakota Elder, and Co-Founder of the Non-Profit Running Strong for American Indian Youth**

"It is a rare thing to see from inside a young woman's spiritual journey, even rarer to understand it in all its sensual manifestations, but that is exactly what Lyric Benson Fergusson gives us with *French Kissing God*. And rightly so, for what is more life affirming, what should awaken your very core more than a spiritual awakening? From the blush of first love found in 'Maybe After Dinner' to the powerful rhythmic churning of 'Wake-Up Calls,' Ms. Benson Fergusson runs the gamut of feelings about falling in love with God, in whatever form that takes for you. A refreshing and original road map to one's journey of enlightenment." ~ **Angelina Fiordellisi, Producing Artistic Director at the Cherry Lane Theatre, New York City**

"To say that Lyric has led an interesting life is an understatement. She is a force that comes in the form of spiritual pilgrim, astute student, ferocious musician, poet, and beautiful woman. *French Kissing God* is a reflection on all that and so much more. Lyric takes us on a journey through God's mystery, playfulness, and grace through the slinky, sometimes sexy, and always potent poetry that can be delighted upon in this volume. I highly recommend it for any lover of the heart's path. There's enough here to go back to again and again, to possibly share with your beloved or to read as you're going to bed. These poems are such a delight." ~ **Zach Leary, Writer and Yogi**

"In *French Kissing God*, Lyric gracefully reflects the passionate and sometimes turbulent inner dance of the Goddess within each of us." ~ **Sheila Applegate, Award-Winning Author of *Enchanted One* and Founder of the "Be Awesome: Your Guide to Conscious Living" Program**

"As I read through, my heart kept expanding to hold the increasing vibration of 'OH, YES-ness!' Each piece, that NEXT poem, became my favorite until I understood that each piece was part of the wonderful whole, as each one of us is part and parcel of THE WONDERFUL WHOLE. Looking very forward to *French Kissing God*'s release; my loved-ones will truly enjoy this publication and I will relish gifting it to them!" ~ **Melina Carnicelli, Founder of Metatron Travel and Former Mayor of Auburn, New York**

FRENCH KISSING GOD

FRENCH KISSING GOD

~ A JOURNEY TO ENLIGHTENMENT ~

LYRIC BENSON FERGUSSON

Published by
Lyric Benson Fergusson
P.O. BOX 197
Wailuku, HI, USA
96793

Cover design: Rosalie van den Bos
Photo credit: Asher Fergusson

First Edition
ISBN: 0578166682
ISBN 13: 9780578166681
Library of Congress Control Number: 2015911135
Lyric Benson Fergusson, Wailuku, HI

For the unexpected journey that kicked you where the sun don't shine.

For the heart that never stopped believing.

And for God too.

Yes,
that sounds nice.

CONTENTS

PREFACE

We live in a remarkably unusual time. It is a time of mass spiritual awakening juxtaposed with devastating world suffering. Each of us, through how we live and exist in the world, has the opportunity to motivate those around us to live a more awakened life. I hope this book will provide inspiration and bring home the message that enlightenment is a glorious human experience, one that is attainable in this modern age and, humbly, not to be lived without.

The intention of this book is to propel a "love-light revolution" for all who seek awakening—a rallying of souls who see that we are all One, as we truly hold no separation in the eyes of the Divine. To me, God is simultaneously the sunlight beaming through your mother's eye, the horrific stench of piss steaming in a gutter, the missing tooth of an old man, and the last passionate kiss you ever give your lover. It's all bliss.

I hope you can feel the humanity in my poetry, in the rhythmic pattern of my soul. Like a seashell echoing the ocean's roar, that you hear and feel your own soul's powerful voice echo through my words—for this roaring ocean, with its constant ebb and flow, is the roar of the Divine gently shaping our lives.

NOTE TO THE READER

Who is God? How can I know?

To me, God is an experience, an ineffable Presence, a tangible reality. God is the silence beyond words, and every particle of this mammoth, unfathomable Creation.

God is the source, course, and goal of all things. The supreme power of total indescription that dwarfs the mind and humbles the frightened ego.

In my experience, God is simultaneously genderless, formless, beyond description—and quite descriptive. Sometimes God has appeared to me in form (for example, as a "He" or "She"). I have seen God as deities from all religious traditions—as Jesus, the Buddha, Mother Mary, Shiva, and Lakshmi, to name just a few. They're all celestial forms within the tapestry of Divinity that is available to us.

Throughout this book I use "He," "She," and "It" interchangeably to describe God. I also throw in the words like "Self" or "Being" to spice life up a bit.

To me God has shown Itself to be all of these things. I feel it's only honest to my own intimacy with the subject to represent God in all of "Her" or "His" remarkable forms.

God is an experience. Here's a glimpse of mine.

MY STORY

At age nineteen I remember sitting on the bathroom toilet after a series of extremely painful life events not pooping, but praying.

The fact that I found myself trying to pray was laughable. I had never before attempted to communicate with the Divine. I had, however, been living in New York City when the attacks took place on September 11th, and someone very dear to my family passed away in one of the towers. I'd been experiencing debilitating personal and family illness: My father was preparing for his third open-heart surgery. I was in and out of doctor's offices and hospitals with stomach and back pain so crippling that I would often find myself curled up on the floor, unable to move. I was diagnosed with fibromyalgia and told I needed back surgery for five compacted discs, and doctors were urging me to "solve" the problem with pain pills and anti-anxiety medications.

I was horrified at the prospect that I wasn't even twenty and I was being given medications that only masked the underlying challenges. I turned to marijuana, which did dull the pain. But when I was stoned from sun-up till sun-down, I knew this too had become a problem.

I felt kicked in the gut by life, incredibly unsure of the purpose of my existence, and on top of everything, I was informed that my dog Zeus was dying from a strange platelet disease.

Yes, I was having a really bad day.

I was not the most modest 19-year-old. But luckily, in that moment I was humble enough to ask for help. So I asked "God."

Who was God? I had no idea. I didn't even know if I believed in Him/Her. I had never consciously experienced any aspect of a deity. My parents are not religious. I had never been to a church or temple service, other than a handful of over-the-top Hollywood bar mitzvahs. See, where I grew up, the closest thing to God was *Variety* magazine.

But, for some reason, I prayed anyway.

I literally begged God to get me out of the disaster my life had become—a mess that had such overwhelming momentum that I felt it was swallowing me whole. Like a flailing animal *way* too far out to sea (during a hurricane, at night, when the Coast Guard was on holiday), I couldn't comprehend how I could get back to shore.

I promised God I would never use drugs again, that I would devote my life to making myself better. I just needed His (or Her) assistance.

After that night on the toilet, my life completely changed.

Almost immediately, my family moved from Hollywood to the mountains of North Carolina. My dad bought me two beautiful Miniature Jersey cows, and I began looking within to find the cause of my continued emotional and physical suffering.

One day while taking my cows on a stroll down a dirt road, I ran into a woman who happened to be a meditation teacher. About three weeks later, under the guidance of Maharishi Mahesh Yogi, I learned a very powerful meditation technique called Transcendental Meditation (TM). I felt a peace within me that was beyond any joy I had ever known. The insomnia, fibromyalgia, and back pain seemed to disappear as if by magic.

I wanted more.

I had heard about Maharishi University of Management, a small school in the cornfields of Iowa where all the students practiced TM twice daily in a group. A few months later, I found myself knee deep in an Iowa winter. Even though I was freezing, I loved it there. In this lovely place, my heart began to open.

Tragically, that feeling of inner peace came to a halt a month after I arrived, when a dear friend of mine was murdered right in front of me in the university dining hall. We were eating our dinner when, without warning, another student (who was later diagnosed with schizophrenia) stood up, picked up a steak knife, and stabbed my friend in the neck.

Two strong young men pulled the crazed student off him. I remember laying my companion on the floor as I called 911. I'll never forget how time came to a standstill as I held his hand.

He died right there on the cafeteria floor.

That was my breaking point. I had had my fill of the bullshit of life. To me the world was harsh, cruel, and frightening. The only solace I experienced was in the depths of my own consciousness. All I wanted to do was dive within. And, as painful as everything was around me, my soul was finally beginning to free itself. I knew I needed a safe environment in which to unravel.

At the age of twenty-one, I decided to join Maharishi Mahesh Yogi's coherence-creating group for world peace. I learned advanced TM techniques and spent about eight to ten hours a day in eyes-closed meditation.

My life was devoted to silence. I lived as a celibate monk for over eight years, and began unearthing the depths of my soul.

I grew every day. I began to perceive the power of God in every moment. The thick, juicy silence that was so accessible in my meditation began to rule my life—literally *rule* my life.

The kind of Silence that deserves a capital "S" became my constant companion through thick and thin, intense sickness and pain, absolute confusion, and the surprisingly painful aches of spiritual awakening. God's presence remained like a light that would not go out.

My beloved teacher Maharishi Mahesh Yogi commented that my experiences were "Better than any cinema… The peaceful, the blissful, the undivided, that is the Self. *That* is to be known."

I couldn't have agreed more. I'd sit in silence and feel united with the Creator so deeply that it was blissfully excruciating. I would watch God showing me creation in so many beautiful details.

Between meditations I would wash dishes or clean the house, all the while seeing angels flying around my room. Ascended Masters from many traditions began to appear before me, and structures of creation began to unfold before my eyes—when they were both open and closed. These were experiences that I had read about in the Ancient Vedic Literature. I never thought it was possible to have such clarity of cognition at this time on Earth. Yet there I was, being blessed with visions and insights that were beyond my mind's comprehension. Most importantly, the love of God (the Self, Being, or whatever you choose to call pure, all-denominational bliss) was always there.

The highs of my spiritual experiences were unprecedented, yet something very strange began happening to my physical body. My digestion got incredibly weak, I lost a massive amount of weight, and my body began shaking uncontrollably. It was so strange to have powerful experiences of God and, simultaneously, a total lack of integration within the body.

At a certain point I suffered what some would describe as a "Kundalini blowout," wherein my nervous system wasn't capable of handling all the spiritual energy, or Shakti, that was flowing through me. I had to leave the meditation group. My body was beaten to a pulp. At five foot four I only weighed ninety-five pounds, I could hardly walk up a flight of stairs, and my body would spasm violently throughout the night.

I remember lying on the floor the day of my twenty-fourth birthday, my body shaking so hard I couldn't make it stop, wondering if what I had done to myself was irreversible. It was hard for my small self to reconcile what was happening. How could the very things that brought so much bliss and meaning to my life be tearing my body apart?

This is how life taught me the power of the Middle Path, as the Buddha so beautifully described it: a path not of extremities, but of balance.

Luckily, after visiting a handful of very perplexed doctors, I sought guidance from my parents and spiritual healers and teachers Matthew Reifslager and Carol Hardin, who helped begin re-anchoring me within my physical body.

The damage that the Kundalini blowout had done to my body was immense. It affected my mind, my body, and my senses. There was not a particle of me that was not torn apart by this great transformation. It took me more than four years to fully recover.

What's remarkable is, throughout this painful healing process, the infinite Silence of God was always holding me, guiding me, and healing me. Clearly kissing my wounds. With the assistance of so many loved ones, I climbed my way back to God's door over and over again, humbled each time. My body and mind were being rebuilt, my nervous system was growing powerful enough to integrate the tremendous amount of Kundalini energy pouring in, and my soul (or higher Self) was beginning to speak through my voice.

During this four-year healing process, I began to write. Even when I could hardly sit up because of my extreme fatigue I would write. I would spend hours creating love songs to God, expressions of the beauty and dirt that was unearthed within me.

This experience showed me what it was like to be truly weak. And in that weakness I fell upon God, and somehow God's ocean became me.

I realized life is not something to be feared, but rather embraced, no matter the circumstances. I became whole. Healthy. Full of love. I began to discover how universal compassion truly begins with self-acceptance. How humanity breeds divinity, and divinity humanity. How God is ever present in pleasure and pain.

I have over 2,000 poems written in His/Her honor.

Enlightenment is the ultimate path. Sometimes it's unexpected. It might lead you places you've never dreamed of. In my humble experience it is, at times, extremely challenging, because you are swimming in such a different current than the rest of the world. But life is often challenging anyway. So you might as well hold God's hand through the process.

Once your grip is tight around God's palm—and you feel the heat of His fingertips as your own—everything becomes so strikingly beautiful.

Because God is you, and your love is God. Everything. Everything. Everything.

"And, what is 'God', anyway?"

Oh right, God is everything.

No matter how overwhelming life may seem, if you strive for light in every moment, love will permeate even the deepest wound. You will be at peace in the challenge and watch as mountains turn to pebbles at your feet, because you grew that damn big.

I have learned an immense amount on this journey, and I have so much inspiration to share. I hope you enjoy the ride!

1
FALLING IN LOVE

GOD'S FRENCH KISS

Last night God offered me a kiss…

Of course I accepted!

I could never deny such a handsome being as He.

Side effects?

I began experiencing uncontrollable affection
for every creature I could see…
Then, I was warned by some flirtatious angelic onlookers
that sudden and/or gradual death of the ego is expected,
lack of verbal communication with others, reclusive behavior,
fits of uncontrollable laughter, excruciating bliss,
and possible mental confusion might occur
as my life crumbles like pebbles,
from a disintegrating mountain
to my feet.

Hmmm…
They never mentioned this in the storybooks.

All in all, those amorous heavenly beings were right.
It was an intense night,
let me tell you.

But by morning I found the sun kissing my toes
requesting me to stir.
Wiping the sleep from my eyes,
feeling quite transformed,
I regained awareness and realized
that God was standing by my bedside
asking me to use my newly revised tongue to speak.

To enlighten this earth with the playful words
of my own cosmic sunshine.

Hmmm… quite a task.

Especially for one little being,
sitting up in bed,
slightly disoriented,
and recovering from God's crazy
(surprisingly juicy)
kiss.

Honestly, I almost declined.
But then, I began to feel something flopping dramatically around in
my mouth,

and I realized…

My tongue has become quite powerful.

"Wow!" I exclaimed.
"What an honor, to birth my love into this world
through words."

"Yes," He said,

"For You have consumed God's cosmic breath.
And all of life is born from here."

Well, I thought, "It's a good thing You brush your teeth often."

Then with a smile God remarked,
"Would you like another French Kiss?"

How could I decline such an offer?

Equally Relentless

Sweet one...

God's love is relentless.

How He will churn the ignorance out of you,
by dragging you across star-fields
by your pinky toe,
howling,
until you finally surrender.

The heat of the stars burning through pride.
The rings of Saturn can be quite cutting, let me tell you.

I know, I have been there...

I throw specks of dust from my journey onto paper,
in hopes that they will spark and catch fire in your heart,
and light fire to this world too.

Until all of our love
becomes
equally relentless.

God Is All Genders. Now, Woo Me.

My Beloved knows me well.

God used Her most mischievous moves
to woo me.

She even sent Him to catch my eye.

His batting eyelashes and dark skin,
smelling of sandalwood,
has caught my attention.

Quite sexy is He, dancing in and out of Her flames,
beckoning me in.

It's a choice to jump wholeheartedly into God's fire,
and She knows I am not without desires.

For even while I'm ablaze with light
I'll dream of Him running His hands across my form.

Quite a magician God is,
because when I leapt into the flames,
intoxicated by my Love's enchanting 'bod,'
the fire's purification became so strong
I could not remember what my human mind even wanted!

(Was it a 'He,' 'She,' or 'It'?!)

And POOF!

Fearless union,
in the bonfire of God realization.

That's the whole story, really.

When existence is seen only as God's love,
no gender is left,
and yet everything in this Universe (and all others) remains.

What a lovely place to be!

God revealed Herself to be Him
God revealed Himself to be It.
God revealed It to be nothing at all.

Yes, I was wooed into God's sweet fire,
where I realized
I had unequivocally wooed my Self.

Your Heart

Censor your heart, love,
and you'll live as the dead live.

There is not a moment
of your life
that is
unholy.

Maybe After Dinner?

God,
it is the halfling in me
that still feels a bit embarrassed
to be standing naked before You.

You see,
I am bearing my soul to You—
taking away the covers
and there is some vulnerability there, yes?

So please be gentle when You come.

For my mind believes
we do not know each other well enough
for You to...

just
yet.

I am simply not accustomed to such a union.

But, when You run Your hands softly against my chest and galaxies
emerge...

Or when You breathe into my ear and I hear the whole ocean
roaring...

Or when you gaze into me with Your giant sparkling eyes,
dancing with starlight,
and oozing with love…

I find myself wholly intoxicated.

So,
considering I am quivering
with visible anticipation
as You inch Your way near,

I think I could make an exception—just this once.

Maybe after dinner?

(wink, wink)

WORSHIPPED YOU BEFORE

I've worshipped You before.

I've laid across Your form.

I recognize Your face…

Those eyes…
Those lips…

I've knelt before You,
as You softened my tears.

Was it within the woods—below moss-drenched trees?

A mosque?

A temple?

A church?

Pray,
tell me.

What other lives have led me here?
(Mysterious as they may be.)

God,
I know I have seen You before.

I would recognize Your face
anywhere.

Every Time We Kiss

Our souls unite every time our eyes meet.
We consume each other,
becoming one.

Our soft,
precious undulations
give rise to divine flow.

How we yearn so deeply for God in this most tangible embrace.

We almost taste God's precious lips on our own…

That is what we get,
every time

we
kiss.

The Sore Parts

My guru once said,
"Give me all your thorns."

So, knowing His Grace,
I threw every last one into the fire.

Not realizing there were quite some left
on my backside
and in places where the sun don't shine.

Hmmm....
What to do?

How can I rid myself of that which I do not know exists?

And yet,
I knew there was something amiss.

So,
I asked my Beloved
to kiss all those places I could not see.

To save me the anguish
of plucking
one

right after
the
other.

(A process quite excruciating, love—
and let me tell you, it takes quite some time.)

So He did—

God's soft lips
made each painful hidden spot
so holy, too.
Every sore is now beaming with light.

He did this
so that I might not hide
even one speck
of me.

And I reveal it *all* to you, love...

All the soft, sweet, juicy,
delicate, pink
and tender parts.

And the scars,
as rough,
thick, and unkind
as untreated leather.

We all have these hidden places,
love.

And to Him, they are light too.

Even the sore parts,

they are
God
too.

Your Dog's Flea

God says, "All is God!"
"God is God, is God, is God."

He doesn't seem to mind at all that the forms of god often have fun,
getting dressed up, wearing each other's clothing.

He is She.
She is 'It'—
and 'It' is He *and* She… apparently.

What more can be said?

When the sky dances with angels and the clouds sparkle in my
vision,
why does it really matter if God has breasts
or a giant moan-maker between His legs?

God is *me*.
God is *She*.
God is *He*,
'It,' and *your dog's flea*.

So,
my love,
I just let it Be.

— 19 —

SWALLOWED

Can I be
swallowed
by You,
Love?

Please… ?

You split the sea inside my heart,
and there is quite a gap there.

Two turning walls of light,
moving in Your direction.
My chest has become a playground
of Your love.

A hand
deep inside my chest
spinning.

Your hand
deep inside my chest
churning.

My soul
deep inside Yours
aching

to be
One.

Union…
is this inevitable?

God says,
"I am
already
here.
Where is there to go?"

CATCHES MY AWARENESS

My inner hands work like elves before sunrise,
never sleeping.

The Goddess catches my awareness
and keeps it as Her own.

My Self emerges
everywhere.

I feel God dancing in my cells.

What a beautiful night!

For there is nothing more
that I wish for
than freedom.

The freedom
of knowing God's form
within my own.

A Saint's Peace

In love I sit,
an overwhelming silence, where His grace takes form.

A mountain,
nested in a valley,
cradled in the illusion of space and time.
All in His love.

All in God's love.

Form after form.
So transcendental
the vibration of depth and peace,
calling out,
" ... "

Nothing,
no-thing-ness.

Radiating from my heart,
waves of devotion crash like untamed wolves
penetrating the ocean of pure
transcendental Being.

In Your grace.

There is no reason to escape.

For I am one.
Peace.

Settled.
Even in this
most physical
form.

LIVE AS YOUR HEART LIVES

Where your mind wavers,
your heart overcomes.

Your heart can tame any monster,
your heart can devour any fear.

Your heart's chivalry is incomparable.

Your heart's genius
outsmarts what's written on parchment
or etched on stone tablets.

Your heart sees an ogre
as an angel,
just waiting to be born…
(with a soft kiss.)
Are you brave enough to pucker up?

Your mind would rather run from sleeping tigers
who had,
several decades ago,
promised to eat you,
than face the unknowns of life.

Your heart knows
overwhelming darkness

is a miracle
waiting to happen.

Which lens do you choose to see this world through?

Your heart, or your mind?

Baby,
it's all about perspective.

NAKED BEFORE TRUTH

My enthusiasm for Truth is unimaginable to naked eyes.
(as *lovely* as they are)

So I choose to lay naked before Truth
so it may cloak me
in Its structure.

I am my Self here,
unmoved,
yet fully formed.

Sweet and dripping,
with the Silence and power of
God.

Rumbling deep within my soul,
I feel something emerging…

She says,
"If you choose to crash fully on this earth,
your heart will soften its descent."

"Like Lord Shiva's hair,
catching the Ganges,
smiling."

Phew.[1]

---

1   There is a story in the Vedic Literature explaining how Lord Shiva saved the earth
from being crushed by the powerful impact of the Ganges River as it flowed from the
heavens. The Ganges, unparalleled in its power and strength, is considered to have
been birthed by the ocean of pure consciousness. The gods feared that if it were to hit
Mother Earth it would surely cause the planet's destruction. Because of this, Lord Shiva
volunteered to sit under this great force and allow his hair to break the fall. To Lord
Shiva, this power that would have broken Mother Earth to bits was nothing. He is often
depicted as sitting peacefully with eyes closed under the flow, absorbing the impact,
and allowing the river to trickle down his hair and safely onto Mother Earth.

In this poem, I am likening the power of individual soul-consciousness to the river
Ganga, and my heart to Lord Shiva. For our heart is the only tool we have that can fully
embrace the unstoppable force and dynamism of our Being.

2

AWAKENING

I Am That

I open my self
to Earth energy,
I feel it flow,
setting me free.

As I breathe in the light
I'm exploring dimensions
morning, noon, and night.

I give my soul to love's Cosmic Cuisine
'cause I am That
which can and cannot be seen.
I am That
which can and cannot be seen…

I'll always remain,
there are no words to explain
how I am the earth, wind, thunder, and rain.
I melt in the gap,
let go of desire,
as I feel the vibrations
of heavenly fire.

I give my soul to love's Cosmic Cuisine
'cause I am That
which can and cannot be seen.
I am That
which can and cannot be seen…

Ya heard me—
I am That
which can and cannot be seen.

Woo!

Gaia![2]

I feel the Earth inside of me.
I can't describe this ecstasy.
We can change humanity.
I'm suddenly serene—
'Cause I am That which can and cannot be seen.
I am That which can and cannot be seen.

---

2   Gaia is another word for the powerful creative force that is Mother Earth.
Get a FREE download of this song at www.FrenchKissingGod.com/Gifts
From the album *Lyric's Love Light Revolution*. All songs by Lyric Benson and Robby
Benson.

I've gone deep,
deep into the Self.
My eyes have wept
from the celestial wealth.
I had the courage to return.
Why don't ya join me—there's karma to be burned.

I give my soul to love's Cosmic Cuisine,
'cause I am That
which can and cannot be seen.
I am That
which can and cannot be seen.

Yes,
I am That
which can and cannot be seen...

Woo!

So Holy

Today,
all of life became so Holy.

Every particle.

Even my shit became
so damn Holy.

STORY

The human body is vast,
far beyond what the eyes can see.
With many layers, dimensions, and forms.

So many intricacies, it's hard to keep up, really.

With all the complexities of your human form,
how is it that your body is a speck,
on a freckle, of the higher Self?
Even time bows to your eternal You.

This is what you are.

Not a body, but a *Being.*

This is where
the story
begins.

Mother Earth

Mother Earth,
a breeding ground for life.

Listen…
She moves,
doesn't She?

Whispering softly,
"Come home…"
"Come home…"

How could it be so long since I remembered the place of my birth?

Then the soul erupts in tiny murmurs,

"Listen…"

Her voice again comes…

"It is all light."
"It is all God's light."

Howling is this Earth's silence,
beckoning me home.

LUCKY

Delicate green shoots trampled
by eager feet
yearning for God,

quickly replaced by sprouting
jungles,

leaves as large as elephants' heads.

I lie on the ground where God dwells.

Lucky,
God dwells
everywhere.

So Tasty

Your silence birthed Creation.
Yet, it remains silent, ever still.

It's an explosive effortlessness
you will learn to call
home.

Isn't it so deeply satisfying?

That Creation could be born within?

Yes, love.
Yes, it is.

Isn't it
delicious?!

ALWAYS MORE

I watch:

Sunrise.
Sunset.

Sunrise.
Sunset.

Events orchestrated by celestial beings constantly pulling the strings
of creation.

Now, I've experienced:
What the senses of this earthly body perceive
is never the whole story.

Close your eyes, love.

There is always more to discover
within.

Make Love Here

God,
I see you everywhere.

Emerging in great beams,
the ground illuminated,
enkindled by Your spectacular light.

The demi-gods dance here,
make love here,
birthing universes
effortlessly from their pinky toes.

Your love's light shines
upon this ground.

Open your eyes to it
and see
the loka
this Earth
has now become.[3]

---

3   Loka is a Vedic term for a heavenly world, or higher dimensional reality.

CLIPPED WINGS

A fig tree outside my window has begun elucidating
the magic of its most subtle forms.

I wonder what remarkably fantastic creatures
will begin speaking to me,
now that Mother Earth has regained her
once clipped
wings.

Maybe we will all
begin to
fly!

The Beloved's Sparkling Eye

My silence…
I am consumed by it.
I am swallowed by it.
I am awake in it.

As I am awake in all things.

All fear,
all weakness,
all mistrust,
all discontent,
disappears.

Consumed are my mind's mischievous creations
by this great force of divine light.

Their embers belly dance,
illuminating the night sky as stars,
twinkling in the depth
of my Beloved's sparkling eye.

Being of Light

A being of light you have become.

This physical structure morphed,
becoming compatible with the spirit
hidden within.

This immortal Soul watches as the body transforms.

Infinite wisdom whispers
into the mind—
revolutionizing it,
enlivening it.

Humbly it sits.
Open and awaiting silence.

So it may too hold infinity
in its crystal goblet.

THIS IS ODD

God's laugh is so delicious!

It's an uproarious,
melodious,
kind,
caring,
loving
voice

coming from…
coming from…
coming from…

within?

Wait.

Is that My voice?

Well, this is odd…

Not So Bad

We've been caught
dancing on God's
sweetly scented
fingertips.

As rose-colored glasses emerge
from our
ravenously delicious
union,

somehow life looks
"Not so bad."

SOUL SPEAK

How does the Soul speak?

In words?
In music?
In dance?
In love?
In soft, *inappropriate* laughter…?

In anything it can get its hands on these days,
that brings light
into your eyes.

FIND THE LOVE

Your body exists.

And then it goes.

Your body exists.

And then it goes.

Your body exists.

And then your body goes.

It moves, love.
This whole creation moves in infinite transience.

Gazing above,
one moment here,
the next moment gone.

The preciousness of this life is unimaginable.
The details of this life, so unique and intangible.

Love dances in every given situation.
Feed it to yourself,
for infinite saturation.

Juice love from every moment.
Serve it to others.
Let your love drip down their lips like succulent candy.
How handy, when you lick it off them, like sweat off your longing
lover.
The perfect atonement.

Why not?

Your body exists.
And then it goes.

Your body exists.
And your body goes.

Feed the world your kindness.

Don't be shy....
When will you see them again?

Next time, surely we won't look the same.

(wink, wink)

3

THE LION ROARS

THE WORD GOD

"God."
(excuse me as I clear my throat.)

"God... "

Could a word as pure as sunlit pools
be soiled by the minds of man?
Yes, love.
In some cases "God" has.

Wipe it clean.

It is a choice:
When to wield the Word, like a sword,
with power beyond compare.

A Word that ignites its meaning,
no matter how hidden the essence is
within the folds, of the hearts,
of those lovers of Self.

Yet, I find
the density of this world
bears fruit without meaning
for most.

My brothers have bled, my father has cried,
I have touched the face of a dying man,
and I have seen a child birthed before my very eyes.
I have been so ill, painfully weak,
I could hardly move.
Yet, I clawed my way to His feet,
again and again,
as I refused to see another
before He
looked me
in the eye.

Even in the horrors
that threw false shadows before me,
even in pain,
even in sorrow
churning so deep within,
that I was unable to move,
or relinquish the concept of what may have happened
upon the landscape of this earth,

I have felt God's love.
And I have seen God's love.

I have seen Her light permeating even there…
Dancing like fireflies beneath the screen of the Self.

Although this contradiction has been shocking to the smallness of
my mind,
the wholeness of every moment can only be perceived.

I have become so accustomed to God's company
that there is no turning back—
For this is how I expect to live.

Angels dance before me now.
Yet there is so much more work to be done.

God is everywhere.
Even there, love.
Somehow, I see God there.

I use the Word.
I *feel* the name's meaning as best as my soul can, as best as my love can.

Your love knows the nuances well.
We speak the same language.

The universe is not blind. The universe is all encompassing.

And yet
we must acknowledge,
as even those in Union know,

God makes
many pieces
out of the One.

FRAGMENTATION

Love for God is breaking me.

In this state of supreme severance,
my identity shifts,
and I am the Self,
without form
at all.

THE DELUGE CAME

I thought
it was about to be
clear,

then a deluge came

washing away all memory
of "me."

Now I am an empty vessel.

Raw.
Open.

Unmoving,

and deeply vulnerable.

The aftermath of a great storm,
when the fields are revealed to be nothing
but the earth itself.

Life is at a standstill.

A deep quiet fills my soul.

I ask,
"What will You fill me with now, God?"
"Now that I am nothing but bones and skin."

"What divine elixir
will You fill me with,
to make my heart worth beating?"

SHE HAS TEETH

I am about to bear my soul to you.

Watch out.

She has teeth.

You see, lust,
pure animalistic desire…

If I were to run
my tongue
across your
heated,
dripping,
swollen body…

Would I not be as holy?

Grace touches me in all ways.

In all ways.

Use your imagination, love.

That's what it's here for.

ROARING IN STILLNESS

Roaring is She

who sits alone
in stillness.

For silence is not so silent.

As distant hums
soon turn to universes
whirling
in empty space.

Fly Against the Window

Ah, mind…

Even the fly
dancing across the windowpane
needs Love's hand
to open the door

and set
him
free.

GASPS

Drowning in sorrow,
overcome by confusion,
the troubled mind
GASPS—

begging
to be awakened.

It's like a breathless child,
calling for its Mother.

AGAINST THE WAVES

You have thrown yourself against the waves, love.
Can't you see? They are breaking against you.
And you are breaking too.

Breaking.
Broken.
Lost.
Found.

An ocean you are becoming—when there is nothing left of your
smallness here.

Painful as it may be.
Inevitable as it may be.

But as you expand across the night sky,
with wings as thick as pure no-thing-ness,

a sweet peace forever reminds you
coming home really wasn't
"All that bad."

Take a breath, love.
Remember: your soul is awakening.

What a powerful creature you have become.

LOVE STINGS

Love stings
like antiseptic
against the troubled mind.

Reactive as it may seem,
the mind often acquiesces
to the heart's
subtle
charms.

(As She is
quite enticing.)

Smoldering love
quickly melts fears gold over flames,
and transforms them
into something
all that more
valuable.

You.

THIS HAPPENS OFTEN?

The rain ceased.
Then we drove ten miles into the storm.

Why do we do this, love?

Unease
is
passing.

Why do we ask it to
linger?

One-Legged Sailors

The Earth is a boat on rough waters
and we are a crew of tipsy one-legged sailors—

with one bump
the whole lot of us
goes down.

I jumped ship the other day
and found the wise ones
rocking-out on the bottom of God's ocean.

We looked into each other's eyes
and somehow,
we all became infinite.

It Sticks

This Silence:
more delicious
than a thousand desserts
the mind could devour.

When the mind finds Peace…

It sticks.

When it knows all
is OK:
"Ahhhhh…."

The mind
breathes a sigh of relief,
as it becomes overwhelmingly apparent,
all of its suffering
was indeed
unneeded.

Not Quite Integrated

The many fields of my Being

open.

I am that Self that knows only my Self to be.

And yet,
what am I to do during the day?

The realms that catch my eye are luminous
even in the darkest hours,
but here I must function within
the confines of this most gross manifest reality?

This I find confusing.

Sometimes I wonder why
I am here.

To know Wholeness?
That which I already am?

I function in this Silence,
I speak from here,
I move from this place.

And yet formless has taken a form
that my mind feels I do not fit within.

"Huh?"

My heart expands to touch all realms,
and yet my mind twists and turns, unsettled,
causing much turmoil within the bigness of my Self.

*A giant
taken down by a pea.*

What is the nature of this incarnation?!

I am awake
yet wonder what I'm to do.

So transcendental I have become—
I'm here,
vanishing within the Self,

while standing on this solid ground, unmoved.

All of life has been for awakening,
and now I sit yawning on the side of my bed,
rubbing my eyes—and stepping onto the fields of light before me.

～～

What now?
I ask.

A voice…

"Flow in dharma.[4] In service. In love…"

"Oh yes—*and integrate*, my dear."
"You're not quite there yet."

Lesson?

I should probably continue awakening.
This is the ultimate gesture
to the glory of
the highest Self.

---

4   Dharma is a Vedic term describing a life path that is in accordance with the soul's highest purpose.

Human Am I

Human am I,
afraid and overshadowed.

God am I,
fearless and full of Being.

Two in one...
One in two...

What a strange incarnation
that I live.

Both God and self
exist in Me.

WIPED CLEAN

Break me.

Break me into a million pieces.

Break me until I am dust.

Break me until I am soot.
Until I am nothing,
moving below Love's dancing feet.

(I feel Your toes.)
Up,
down,
left,
right.

It is the gripping that keeps
life from
moving.

Like nails on a chalkboard
the ego screams
when I ask for the slate

to be wiped
clean.

Entangle Me Whole

Your song,
a piercing howl
running through my Being,
sweeping across open plains,
hitting the ghost town in my heart.

Wildly weeping through empty wooden hallways,
sorrow sweeping swollen dust around my soul.
Circling. Encapsulating. Enveloping.
Nothing majestic in this dance.

Yet, so majestic.

Dry air rips You from my lips.

You push me forward,
always releasing me,
before the adulteration of sorrow
is forever obliterated
by the impending deluge of my soul.

When sorrow churns like a wave in Her ocean,
it is immensely powerful to feel,
rather than deny.

Even pain is worthy of God's love.

God I love You.

God I love You.

God, how I love You.

I am so thankful for the journey.

Please.
Entangle me.
Whole.

WITHOUT FORM

Will you hold it against me?
I dove so far into the abyss of Self,
I did not look back,
as my body turned to sand
before you.

Will you hold it against me?
I lost all sense in this great transformation

who was
this "*i*"—?

I was lost
without form
(in my Beloved's arms.)

Will you hold it against me?

That I cannot be
who I once was?
that I cannot bare to be
her—

That I couldn't be
without the Silence and Truth

resonating
inside of me?

A part of me still stings like Hell from this journey.

A part of me still smokes with its memory.
A part of me still feels its excruciating pain.

Tears fall.

What can I say?

Will I hold it against you, love,
that you did not understand then?

Life continues.

And I am stronger
than
I once was.

Everything

Revel in the imperfection
of words.

For nothing spoken
is God.

Except everything
ever said.

IN THE VALLEY OF MY SOUL

In the valley of my Soul,
in the darkness of the night,
I align with that which is pure light.
And in this bliss I do exist,
becoming whole,
deep within my Soul.

The angels come to me and begin to set me free.
I am not afraid—
I'm part of a celestial parade.
Brilliant orange and reds,
and the sun begins to spread.
I'm suddenly embraced by the beauty of Her grace.
Free from all control,
and that makes me
whole—

In the valley of my Soul,
in the darkness of the night,
I become that which is pure light.
And in this bliss I do exist,
becoming whole,
deep within my Soul.

In the valley of my Soul,
in the darkness of the night,

I AM THAT which is pure light.
And in this bliss I do exist,
becoming whole,
deep within my Soul.

The angels come to me and begin to set me free.
I am not afraid—
I'm part of a celestial parade.
Brilliant orange and reds,
and the sun begins to spread.
I'm suddenly embraced by the beauty of Her grace.
Free from all control,
and that makes me
WHOLE. [5]

---

5 **Get a FREE download of this song at www.FrenchKissingGod.com/Gifts**
From the album Lyric's Love Light Revolution. All songs by Lyric Benson and Robby Benson.

— 78 —

WAKE-UP CALLS

Topsy-turvy in life's confusion,
wandering around a great illusion.
Wondering why the people shout,
wondering what it's all about.

Is there a remedy
for horror, pain
and greed?

From anger, it seems,
this world does feed.
We're tumbling 'round on faulty knees,
on tripped-up lines
and broken creeds.
Relying on what our human eyes can see
is constantly re-birthing inaccuracies,
allowing our brothers' souls to bleed,
while feeding them wine from fucked-up trees.

Here I am, a simple wo-man
wandering to my very core,
wondering what life on Earth is for?
I watch the news, feeling sore.
With sacks of lies and misused lore.
Nations founded on blood, guts, and gore—
where truth boils down to a football score.

A world confused and saturated with indignity.
You ask, "What do I see?"
(a tangled web of obloquy)
Optimism falls far from the tree.
No. This cannot be.

This is a lie.

This
is
a
lie.

Yes.
And from this lie my heart does flee.
And into God's heart
I am set free.
Shackles broken by waking souls with sprouted wings—

Listen.

We know the power that our LOVE brings.

We can turn the tides of man-made illusion.
We can save our minds from societal confusion.

All persecution could end in a day, if we listened to what our hearts say. When the voice of love resonates within, the veils that we see become so damn thin.

Love thy neighbor.
Feed thy brother.
Cherish your mother.

Become the light within the night—
and somehow, man, you've got it right.

Simple?

A single act of kindness
has the potential to transform a person's life.

And a single human being
can transform the world.

And on,
and on…

*See how powerful
you are?*

Through a single act,
your love
revolutionizes all of
Creation.

One Sexy Poem

Come, Love.

I feel Your lips
running across
my form.

Come, Love.

I feel the warmth of Your breath
caressing every aspect of my Being.

Come, Love.

I beg You,
as I feel the heat
of love
passion
pure sensuality
draping across my flesh
like silk
running,
running,
running,
through me
Love...

Oh, Love...

Won't You come to me?
Won't You come in me?

So that I may know You
here on Earth,
as well?

An Ocean of Pink Milk

An ocean of pink milk churns in me
moving with waves so great
only the heart can comprehend.

Her love is creating cream and butter for my soul to devour.

I am awakening to God
I am awakening to God
I am awakening to God

and I see Her
everywhere.

Guiding Ships Home

Dark waters churn with the wind.

But, what is lit from within

never
goes
out.

Always guiding the ships home.

Nothingness and Somethingness

The silent sea of transcendental love
manifesting
rises and falls upon my chest,
my heart-center,
like a drum.

God's powerful hands hit the sea,
forming waves thick as space.

My subtle form too
rises then falls,
becoming even more enlivened, full.

A concave pull is formed—
rather than a sea parting, it comes powerfully crashing
into the endless silence
residing in my heart.

My energetic roots,
finally drenched in the power of Divine Love,
expand
through the most subtle vibrations of creation.

My body merges with God…
and yet I am already there.

This bliss
is excruciating.

I feel the vastness of God's presence emerging and submerging—
first in form,
then formless.

My physical body is becoming infinity,
rising out of the translucent gleaming sea of Self.

The flickers, the divine beings, dance in the corner of my eye,
filling the screen of my consciousness.

God, pure divinity, grows
more and more real in my awareness.

I stretch into my Self.
I feel into the corners of Being.

Love for God is the only thought.
The only emotion.

Pure silence brings sheer ecstasy

in loving God, my ocean bows before Life,
as it shows itself to be the totality that I know in my heart.

I am free!

God's Being held space for me as I lost all form; and so did He.

God became nothingness, pure expansion without end, without gender, without form.

My heart, my Being, fills with this supreme nothingness.

Love for God. Love for Self. Love for Being. This is the driving force of Creation.
It is all that remains—when there is something to remain.

Having drunk and now fully intoxicated, the smallness of my Self melts.
The sea falls, and does not rise again.

I am silent.

Melted into nothingness, sitting in silence, watching the fullness of His form emerge again...

The simultaneous nature of creation:
How nothingness and somethingness can exist, in Me.

DISSOLVES

The light of God,
everywhere,
everything.

My mind distinguishes
many colors,
many shapes,
many figures,
many forms,
many breaths,
many prisms…

The perceived stability
of that which never stands still—

This instability
gives rise to life.

God dances and creation moves.

God rests and all is dissolved back
into She.

SHIT EMBERS

Unbelievable as it may seem,
even the bullshit
in this world
is infused with
God's grace.

Ignited
by His hand.
Ablaze
in Her palm.

No matter how stinky.

If you look closely you will see
the shit-embers are
falling to Earth
lighting the path home
to infinity.

Every ounce of life has a purpose.

Even "shit" is there for a reason.

It's asking you to look within.

THE LION ROARS

The lion roars,
I consume the sky,
and all things turn to fire.

What a beautiful morning
just sitting here
with my eyes
closed.

OVERFLOWING

My heart overflows with wisdom…

in loving God
I begin to see
all of Creation.

Great Escape

"What the hell is perfect, anyway?"

Is hell not perfect
in its function
and form?

We spend much time molding ourselves
in attempts to achieve such perfection.

But how can a mind mold
that which it can't even touch?

Poor mind.

Let all concepts of perfection fly
from your
wrestling, swollen belly.

Only in this "great escape"
will Grace flood
the vessel
that is form.

POURING FROM INSIDE

Every mind can misinterpret God's words.
Every mind can confuse God's lyrics.

But every heart speaks God's tongue.

Listen…
and you will hear Infinity
pouring from inside of you.

Let it flow. Fill your goblet.
Become satiated by your internal spring.

It's so sad,
when so many people remain
with empty glasses
upturned toward the sky
waiting for rain.

When so simple is this
sacred knowledge:

"God speaks from within."

EVERY LAST INCH OF ME

The sweetness of God,
as He is loving me…
with dark, deep eyes
twinkling from within.

It is hard to believe
that God, so big,
could love me
so much.

I am a teardrop in His eye,
a hair on His arm,
a particle of His breath.

Yet,
He dances in my heart?
He dances in my soul?
He dances
all over my Being.

As He loves
every last
inch

of me.

BRAHM

The Wholeness of Brahm
surrounds me. [6]
And yet,
a sliver of me remains.

Floating in this Wholeness
an entity—
wondering what it is
still
to become.

Appearing lost on a path
made of open fields.

And here I sit
wondering where God has gone
while climbing on Her belly,
and searching for my own.

Where is this Wholeness
that I find myself swimming in,
that I have never left?

---

6 Brahm is the unchanging reality amidst, and beyond, the world. It is another word
for the wholeness of the highest Self or God.

Where is this Wholeness,
made of the infinite love of God,
resonating like a lyre within my own Being?

Where is this Wholeness?
Where is this God?

Ah, yes...

I am here.
God is here.

I have become Her!

PAUSE

Now that I have uncovered my soul to you in these pages, and you have glimpsed my embarrassing missteps, my divine love life, and my ego-obliterating epiphanies, my hope is that you begin to see so much humanity in the journey of awakening. Love your humanity—it's so divine.

Awakening to God (Self or Being) is an earth-shattering adventure that begins when your heart yearns for transformation and union. When an uncontrollably bright light begins to pierce through you, love you, and wash away everything that is keeping you from knowing the depths of your infinity, you will begin to know yourself, and the Truth that is your nature.

My humble experience is we never leave our humanity behind. Rather, we transform the unique animal that we are into a true expression of our soul.

The human life is the hand that God takes. Once true love exists between self and God, unabashed and blazing, creation will open its heart in unimaginable ways. The angels become constant companions, and the divine beings that preside over creation reveal themselves as the truest, most caring friends.

Human life becomes all that much more exhilarating. We begin to experience firsthand that creation loves us for who we are; for we are so deeply sacred, each soul playing on Earth. God becomes not just something in a church, or on your altar. You have fun with the Divine in all of the dirt and mud that comes with earthly living.

This journey has been internal, but it has revolutionized every drop of my external life. Challenging as life may have been, even overwhelming during times of great illness, I can say with confidence that it is the most rewarding adventure I have ever taken, because the journey is never-ending—and it only keeps getting more exciting!

4

UNTAMED IN LOVE

FOR MY MOTHER

Infinity swirls in her eyes.
Stars are birthed from galaxies in her chest.

Joyousness feeds from freedom jumping in her belly
as her heart whispers to mine,

"Everything we need is found inside..."

A mountain of support
launches spaceships
from the twinkle
in her eyes.

We are one in this knowing,

life is always evolving,
changing...
moving...
in love.

In love.
In love.

All in love.

WILTED FLOWER BLOOMS

Slightly confused
with the purpose of incarnation,

a wilted flower
(beyond all recognition)

begins to bloom.

Sweetly, softly,
nature unfolds.

Wondrous things
begin to be told,

as if nothing
ever happened
at all...

IN FAITH

The one whose knuckles were once clenched white with fear
releases.

Love burns through me
like flames engulfing silk drapes
that block the sun.

I can see a little clearer now.

Fear has no place in my chest.

God holds me,
reminding me that,
in faith,
everything is taken care of.

WITNESS

I dream of the blue-ash color of God's skin
gently brushing against my chest,
turning me to cinders,
yet leaving me whole enough
to enjoy His physical form.

I am falling embers in His hair.

God rebuilds me again, afterward.

Sweet soul,
how I long to witness God's face
in every creature that I see.

Untamed

My awareness floods
like a dam broken by sheer force of current, power, strength.
No woman, man, or beast could tame me.

Let them try.

It is a wonder I remain unmoved…

For an ocean of God froths within me.

As I sit in the sea of my Self,
waiting
for daybreak to come.

SHE'S ALREADY FULL

Can eternity flicker?

I see it in you, love,
like the earth breaking underneath my feet.

A slow
unexpected quiver,
before it cracks,
splits.
Canyons conceived in its tumultuous wake.

Who would have known
such softness could become a light
so piercing,
so silent?

It's streaming from her pores, her eyes, her *Being-ness*.

She is a cavern, a vessel,
for the unmanifest to emerge from.

She is a flame of eternity fanning itself
in the piercing eyes
of a soul
living in dharma.

She hunts,
although she is already full,

in the extreme delicacy of infinite strength budding.

This is you, love.

God, this must be
You…

STOP BLUSHING

I hope to spark
even just one thread
of your filament.

My soul's power, current,
strength and Being
flirtatiously flame
under you.

I see you over there.
Your eyes beg to dance.

It is a wonder we remain unmoved.
The ocean of devotion churning inside us.
The sweat building, percolating on our skin,
the undulating force of God's love surging between our hips,
finally climaxing in an overwhelming,
intoxicating shower of passion
and union within.

Oh, dear...

Stop blushing.
God made me this way.

ANGELS COME, RESTRUCTURING MY HEART

The Goddess churns in Me.

The voice of God moves through my lips—
calling itself my own.

Angels pulling cords of light in all directions.
My breath expands, consuming my Being.

I watch…

Red-gold fire strikes,
beating upon my chest,
as I become the landscape
of a self-created sun.

They are opening me, to God.

Flames of light jump
then are consumed back
into the wholeness of my Godly form.

A ball of fire emerges here,
this light I see,
so tangible in its nature.

My soul's hand reaches,
finally kissing God.

As the tumultuous bliss of celestial fire
consumes
me
whole.[7]

---

7 The above experience was after a particularly deep meditation. I was laying on my
back and watching as hundreds of angelic beings came to my aid, pulling the cords of
creation to assist in my evolution. What I express was happening multi-dimensionally,
not on this very dense realm of creation. Although I did feel my physical body being
deeply affected by this experience.

GREAT AND SMALL

Oh my God,
my love overflows in boundless devotion.

I sit
I stand
I walk
I run
I pray
I become so still...

and You never leave my side,
You never leave my heart.

Vast and unbounded I have become,
for my physiology is where You dwell.

Every inch of me occupied by Your grace,
I am a lighthouse
of Your being,
a flame of the fire
of Your devotion.

My love for You
is in itself immortal.

My love,
My heart,
My God,
I am a droplet, suspended, in the ocean
of Your grace.

Overflowing in tidal waves of inexhaustible bliss,
I love God.

For God is my Self

and
all things
great

and
small.

INTEGRITY

They asked me,
but I couldn't do it.

I thought I would be giving up something.

You.

THE ADVICE OF NOTHING

This now…

This constantly emerging flow
existing omnipresently within the dynamics of my heart.

This unaltered state
of eternal nothingness,
altered by the fluctuations of my most subtle form,

constantly rising in me,
asking me to be
something…

"What will I become today?"

Nothing whispers in my ear.
"Listen."

Shhhhh.
It is speaking
in the form of bubbling ecstasy.

With this,
all I can say is,

"I find it is best
when I am open
to My Own
advice."

5

MY SOUL'S HORIZON

SAID AND DONE

The life of your soul is a journey.
You will never stop evolving.

How can you say
the journey ever ends?

Then again—
creation will someday dissolve
back into itself.

Even Lord Vishnu
must eventually awaken
from His
dream. [8]

Then what is left,
even for Him?

When Vishnu turns over to see
all His universes have returned,
into the depths of God's imagination?

Nothingness remains, love.
Only the Self remains.

---

8   Lord Vishnu is a Hindu deity responsible for sustaining God's creation.

When all is said and done,
only You,
as God,
remain.

INTOXICATING

That which I do not see
is ME.
That which I do not hear
is ME.
That which I have long since feared
is ME.
That which the ego dreads,
the mind cannot comprehend,
is ME.

My body.
My illness.
My painful regrets.
My horrific unthinkable mistakes.
The fear that grips me so twistedly-tight in the belly,
howling into the night… begging me to come "home."

All ME.

(Thank God.)

DANCE
EVERYWHERE
LOVE.

I beg you.

Somehow,
in you,
life expands,

becoming so much more
intoxicating.

WHO?

Someone once said to me,
"Does God exist?"

And I replied,
"Do you?"

How can someone know what they have never touched?

How can someone hold
the very fabric
of their hands?

God lives in me.

God lives in you.

And in you...
And in you...
And in you...
And in you...

And in you...
And in you...
And in you...
And in you...

And in you…
And in you…
And in you…
And in you…

Can you truly experience

G
o
d
?

Can you truly experience You?

Oh love,
of course you can.

Prayer for Stillness

Let me never be without You, God.

Let me never be swallowed
by this smallness of form,
lost in the isolation of my mind,
spinning like a top,
as thoughts of unimportance fly into empty space
screaming, "Here, here, here!"

Never again.

Let me be still, Beloved.
Let me dive into my heart,
and never return.

"Where did she go?"
They ask.

"I am nowhere."
"But I am always here."

Silence does this to you.

Uninvolved and motionless
melted into the pot of my soul,

I sit

until You,
until You, God

ask me
to
dance…

I'm Never Gonna Let You Go

I'm never gonna let You go.

I'm never gonna let You go.

The dark night sky whispers Your name,
I open my heart and I feel no shame.
To be one with Your ash-colored sky,
in our union, my heart can truly fly.

I'm never gonna let You go,
I've climbed love's peak to Your plateau.
With Your love inside of me,
my surrender sets me free.
I'm enlightened and I lose control,
I am gonna consume You whole.

I am Yours from head to toe,
I'm never gonna let You go.

I am Yours from head to toe,
I'm never gonna let You go.

The dark night sky whispers Your name,
I open my heart and I feel no shame.
To be one with Your ash-colored sky,
in our union, my heart can truly fly.

I'm never gonna let You go,
You've filled me up from head to toe.
Some may say this is defeat,
but makin' love is way too sweet.

I'm never gonna let You go,
I'm lost in this turbulent flow,
and as You taste my virgin soul,
You give me strength—
consume me whole.

I am Yours from head to toe,
I'm never gonna let You go.

Never, never, let You go.

I am Yours from head to toe,
I'm never gonna let You go.

Never, never, let You go.

Never, never—

let You go!⁹

9   **Get a FREE download of this song at www.FrenchKissingGod.com/Gifts**
From the album *Lyric's Love Light Revolution*. All songs by Lyric Benson and Robby Benson.

DRIPPING

I am dripping with silence.

For God has kissed me,

and left His mark
all over my Being.

My Soul's Horizon

A silence beyond emotion.
So still...

The wind blowing through my hair:
a display of You,
touching my face in form.

Shhhh....
And then it is gone.

How can fear sustain,
when no outcome but You exists?

No matter the failings,
the mishaps,
the ending ups,
if I have You—if I have *become* You—
there is no other endgame.

This is the purpose of creation.

All other desires wane,
as the dawn of God-realization
ascends
over my soul's
horizon.

DEVI, THE GODDESS

Devi,
stand before me
like the thousand suns of olde.

I rise to my feet
and Your silence becomes me.

I'm pure.
And I'm free.

There's a hush…
Hush…

Then I hear Your peaceful strum.

All at once
my heart beats
to the sound of Your drum.

Come, come,
come, oh Devi.

Come, come,
come and adore me.

In Your arms
I will lie.
'Cause I see the Truth
in Your eyes.

This love explodes like a bonfire of infinite proportions,
and I find it now,
here in life,
consuming fearful distortions.

A personality of mammoth proportions:
The Soul,
the Cosmic Sun,
the lighthouse of Being
leaves me satisfied,
all believing,
all freeing.

Devi,
stand before me
like the thousand suns of olde.

I rise to my feet
and
Your silence becomes me.

I'm pure.
And I'm free.

There's a hush…
Hush…

Then I hear
Your peaceful strum.

All at once
my heart beats
to the sound of Your drum.

Come, come,
come, oh Devi.

Come, come,
come and adore me.

In your arms
I will lie.
'Cause I see the Truth
in Your eyes.[10]

---

10 **Get a FREE download of this song at www.FrenchKissingGod.com/Gifts**
From the album *Lyric's Love Light Revolution*. All songs by Lyric Benson and Robby Benson.

LORD SHIVA'S TREE

This is a tale
about love with a gale-force wind
that whips at your face.

The more that it haunts you,
the more that you want to,
never ever let it
go away.

She is the Wholeness that birthed Creation,
from my light springs all celestial nations.
She is my ultimate liberation,
from the bonds of manifest Creation.

She births the Soul,
and the Soul is me,
giving rise
to this physiology.

A seed from Lord Shiva's Tree
can destroy negativity,
and can also bring
peace,
and love,
and harmony.

And so here I stand,
upon this very land,
with my sword in hand,
obeying Her command:
LOVE, LOVE, LOVE.

Silence…
Love, Silence…

This is a tale
about love with a gale-force wind
as it whips at your face.

The more that it haunts you,
the more that you want to
never ever let it
go away.[11]

---

11 **Get a FREE download of this song at www.FrenchKissingGod.com/Gifts**
From the album *Lyric's Love Light Revolution.* All songs by Lyric Benson and Robby Benson.

I have heard that God appears to His/Her disciples in whatever form will open their hearts and leave the greatest impact. In my experience deities are very real, and very loving. They are benevolent and divine souls that exist on higher realms of creation and help to guide us on our journey.

Lord Shiva is a Hindu deity responsible for the necessary dissolution of ignorance. He has opened my heart so many times in sickness and in health. I am deeply grateful for His unconditional love. Many poems of mine have been written in His honor.

The 'She' I refer to in this poem is the Mother of Creation, standing beyond birth and death and yet giving rise to everything that is and ever shall be. She is a form of the formless all benevolent, all loving, non-judgemental Self.

HIS VOICE

A combustion of life force
flows through
my mind.

My heart
feeds the flames of
Self-love.

Devotion
fuels God's ever-present awareness,
reverberating,
like a chute of light
falling on the river of my Being.

Drop after sacred drop.
The hum of His voice
twirling within me.

Now Taking Form

When will I be ready for my Soul?
When will I look into my eyes
and see Me reverberating there?

I am a child here—
No...
I am now taking form.

I dance here—wildly.

I am on fire with awareness,
as a true form of Me
emerges.

Pure Being
ignited by this cosmic dance,
I shake my head from side to side
and pound my feet
against
the floor
of God's temple
like all other untamed souls
who came before me
who knew TRUTH, GOD, and SELF are ONE.

I am begging you—join me
here.

Nothing is greater than the Self.
Nothing is more untamed than your infinite awareness.

Nothing is more naked than you in love with God,
curled up,
becoming one.

ROMANCE

Will my God incarnate here?

I will wait.
My patience stretches far.
I do not compromise.

As my chest forever pounds,
only
to the beating
of His drum.

His Lips

Silence sweeps over me,
like His lips,
sweeping over my open form.

I unfold myself to Him.

And He finds fields of light,
begging Him to dance.

God, make love to this form.
Sweep away and clear…

I love You with all my Being.

I am a giggling schoolgirl
whose mind is forever occupied
with the vision of Your fire-filled eyes opening

right after we

kiss.

Expression

How can I express God's beauty in form?
My words…

they lose all meaning
the moment they touch
the page.

6
COMING HOME

LETTERS

A poet's words
hold space for God's light.

Characters on a page
act as an excuse
for my Beloved's silence
to dance
explosively
in form.

It's Inconceivable!

Yes Beloved, I am here always!

Let me know how to move.
I promise I will follow with head bowed
so deep in devotion
that I will only see Your shoelaces,
or Your sun-colored toes,
as You walk by.

And, as a gesture of humility,
I will remain with my eyes forever downcast,
just looking at the dirt under my feet.
I won't look up even once, I swear!
All I see is You.

No matter if I am blessed with the privilege of glancing
into Your benefic eyes,
I shall always be satisfied.

And yet, and yet!
I lay before You with eyes so tightly shut
and all I see is Your face illuminated,
a golden sun before me,
so bright!

No matter how downcast these eyes are
You drop below me, again and again and again,

I simply cannot escape Your love.
It's inconceivable!

My mind whirls with thoughts of deep devotion.

So sweet You feed me this way.
Fed from the swirling flames of love
ever established
in
my heart.

He Speaks

There is so much silence in God's love.

I am amazed
how eloquently He speaks

without saying anything

at all.

WHO YOU ARE

Vast and unbounded you are.

For you are where God dwells.

A drop in God's ocean
creates tidal waves
of inexhaustible bliss.

A flame of God's fire
is in itself
immortal.

You are already lit up
from within.

Just being still,
you shine
so bright.

Nothing more is needed…

So, time to get started, yes?

Go on.
Life is waiting for you.

This is who you are.

You are God,
in form.

CHOOSE TO COMPOST

If you choose to poop on my words,
my love will turn your excrements
into fertilizer
that will nourish the plants
and feed thousands.

Great cities will be built
as a direct result
of your bowels.

My love is that transformational.

And so is yours.

Look at what the Beloved does
with a little manhandling.

He is just very resourceful—
nothing goes to waste.

So the next time criticism arises,
simply choose
to compost.

No Longer Closed

What is the purpose of life?

When the eyes
are no longer

closed?

LET'S LIVE LIFE IN PEACE

Calling all extraterrestrials,
homo sapiens,
heteros and homosexuals,
intergalactic multi-dimensionals.

We're all the same crust,
the same dust.
That's who we are—
from the same ancient star.

So have no fear.
Make it loud so all can hear.

LIFE IS OUR FEAST.

So let's

LIVE LIFE IN PEACE.

My big-bellied Love,
ruler of galaxies above.
You come to me in dreams,
proving nothing is as it seems.

So have no fear.
Make it loud so all can hear.

LIFE IS OUR FEAST.

So let's

LIVE.

LIFE.

IN PEACE.

Let's live life in peace!

Nothing is as it seems.
Nothing is as it seems.
Nothing is as it seems.

Let's live life in peace!

I tap the ultimate courage within—
Not necessarily residing under,
within, or throughout my skin—

Moving into action my heart pounds with speed,
as all cosmic energy proceeds.
Into a state of supreme satisfaction:

fearless traction,
tearless reactions.

As we all acquiesce to the power that unites,
and will address
that there is no need to fight,
where we are all one
despite the obvious
black and whites.

Where no matter what nation
we are from,
we can all beat the same
peaceful drum.

Brave, unclothed,
and unashamed,
with no one to blame,
just LIFE to reclaim.

Remove the fear.
Remove the fear.

This is the road in which peace appears.

Calling all extraterrestrials,
homo sapiens,
heteros and homosexuals,
intergalactic multi-dimensionals.

LIFE IS OUR FEAST.
SO LET'S LIVE LIFE IN PEACE.

Let's live life in peace!
Let's live life in peace!
Let's live life in peace!

That's who we are,
from the same ancient star.
So have no fear,
make it loud so all can hear.

Life is our feast.
So let's live life in Peace.

PEACE!!!![12]

---

12 **Get a FREE downloads of Lyric's music at www.FrenchKissingGod.com/Gifts**
From the album *Lyric's Love Light Revolution*. All songs by Lyric Benson and Robby
Benson.

LIKE MALE PIGEONS

How this love aches!
Every cell in me expanded,
puffed up like male pigeons
during mating season,
in springtime,
trying to impress You
while simultaneously stealing bread crumbs from Your lunch—

God, I sit below You hoping to be pummeled by a rainstorm of Your
light
falling from Your lap of cosmic, ecstatic proportions,
begging endlessly
"Where is the sea?!"

I sit.
And yet, and yet…
this form contains Me.

A vortex so concrete pulls every thought, emotion, and feeling
back and back
into the seemingly endless cavern that is my heart!

I have infinity within Me.
My head drops in humility
acknowledging the vastness of Your form

that resides just below... below...
(not that low...)

and all my energy floods this expanding ocean,
and all that I ever wished for simply fades away...

Dear God, dear love,
has love become you yet?

Dear love, dear life,
have you become?

I love you.

Has God become you,
yet?

A MEAL GOD COOKED

My eyes cannot miss it.
My heart cannot beat without God's hand on my drum.

My soul cannot wait to consume this love whole—
to taste it in my mouth,
and call it its own.

… delicious!

That is what "LIFE" is.

The Self is the meal God cooked.

I stir this pot—
and all of Creation
emerges.

APPROPRIATE TO SHARE?

I slurp the liquor of the Gods,
as they feed it to me
through my Being.

Dripping. Oozing.
Formless. Golden-goodness.

So tasty.

When I'm sweetly intoxicated
and slightly tipsy,
the Gods tell me all their secrets.

Like
how the angels rise the sun
with strings.

And all of creation
is a net
in God's fishing boat.

And our heart holds
within it
God's sails.

And God's brig
is a dream,
in the twinkle
of
our
Self's
eye...

After I finally come to,
gently hung-over by my bliss
and slightly exhausted from a night out with the Divine,

I often wonder
if all these
gooey golden secrets

are actually,
in all honesty,

appropriate
to share?!!

ISN'T IT REFRESHING

God is all-accepting.

Shouldn't we be,
too?

Feel into that, love.

Isn't it refreshing?

Until You Fly Somewhere Else

Permanence is disguised
in the impermanence
of this changeable reality.

Points of action fade
into a union more divine
than your mind could have ever imagined.

Impenetrable God,
unchanging,
flickers in your eyes,

until this life
finally ends,

and you
choose to fly
with God
somewhere
else.

Inside a Lotus Flower

He took me in His arms,

and we made love
inside
a lotus flower.

How gentle is He,

that God,
who sustains creation.

BOUQUET OF FLOWERS

God is so far beyond my comprehension.

I am always astounded
when He comes
laughing...

Offering me
a bouquet

of freshly

hand-picked
flowers.

THE SEEKER

Beloved,
God has kindled a fire
in your heart.

Your bonfire
glows bright in this world.

I see it in your eyes.

Flames dance
in deep orbs.

They are fed by His words
whispering in your ear,
reminding you
of the agreement you made
long before
you birthed your self
here.

Beloved,
God has lit a fire in you.

Like a phoenix
you will rise

guiding the others home.

Always in Heat

Have you ever noticed
how animals during mating season
make the strangest noises?

Yelping to the night sky,
wrestling around madly,
gesticulating each other near?

It's an interesting go at romance.

I heard a moose doing just that.
Her song was nearly excruciating.
A bellow of true, unadulterated yearning!

Gave me the chills, really.

Then,
it made me think.

No wonder I am wildly howling at the sky
rolling about,
and truly,
absolutely crazy.

For I am always in heat,
when God
is around.

(And God is always around.)

LIKE BUTTER ACROSS GALAXIES

My Being spreads,
like butter across galaxies,
nourishing all things that come across my beautiful form.

I get cozy in this body's chair,
where a granule of Me resides.

I snuggle deep into its corners,
moving myself around.

Getting comfortable.

WISHING FOR GOD

The sweetest company I have ever found
came through the eyes
of one
wishing for God.

THE LIONESS

God is a lioness.

Humanity acts as a thousand zebras
running away
from their impending consumption.

Don't they know?

It's within the lion's belly
that ultimate liberation
exists.

Lucky are those who are clever enough
to get caught—

cornered,
by a wild pack
of
She.

For within God's belly-fire
is alchemy.

And in a flash,
they are
re-birthed
anew.

Just as the food you eat
becomes the flesh under your skin,

so do you
become God,

when you leap
between
Her teeth.

WHAT'S DIFFERENT?

Did anything change?

Did the external world honestly change that much?

No.
Not really.

I changed.
I transformed.

Now my life is astonishingly
different.

PRAYER, CHILD OF LOVE

Goddess of life,
Goddess of love,
indweller of my soul,
I bow down to you.

I open to You, and receive all blessings.

Thank You for this life,
thank You for Your love.
I am eternally grateful.

I see You as the heart of my life.
I see You as the heart of my soul.

Thank you, God.
I am eternally grateful.

For
God has birthed a child in me,
and that child
is my love.

AFTERWORD

Y ou have the potential to make life an epic journey, one that is worthy of the gift that is your heart. Each moment, each breath—this is your enlightenment. It is the freedom we all crave so deep within us that our hearts salivate for it.

I urge you to find truly humble enlightened teachers, practice meditation, and experience the power of your Self. Be with God barefoot in nature, live in natural environments, and eat fresh foods high in "prana" (life force). Ground and root your body to Mother Earth; the light of this glorious planet will infuse your body with Her heavenly awakening vibrations. Speak your Truth with astounding clarity, be courageous, live from the heart, stay rested, and do what brings you bliss.

You are the highest Self—*Being*—reverberating beyond all the layers of complications that bind us. If you have the intention to live this way, Nature will guide you. Miracles will show you your way.

No soul is born on this Earth fully enlightened. All the beloved spiritual giants such as Raam, Jesus, Buddha, Moses, and Mohammed went through a powerful transformation before reaching ultimate liberation.

Saints, Bodhisattvas, and prophets are people, too. Once we realize this, we can glimpse the paramount potential of our own human life and begin stepping up to the task.

By listening to my heart I found clarity and life's greater purpose. I have shared glimpses of my journey with you in these pages, and there is so much more to come.

If you feel lost on your path, or need inspiration on the journey, my hope is that you can pick up this book as a reminder of the power that dwells within. Because God is already within you. You are already God. The bliss of your silence is beyond words.

God's cosmic joke is that enlightenment isn't really the journey anyway. Life is the journey. Enlightenment is one glorious step on the road of this incarnation. It's the step right before the next step, and the next.

We are each here to walk this earth as unconditional love, acceptance, compassion, ineffable courage, and bliss, which is the essence of humanity's true nature. Never sell yourself short. You are God in human form.

Enjoy the journey.

With all love, light, and luck on your way,
Lyric Benson Fergusson

ACKNOWLEDGEMENTS

My darling Asher! You are my lighthouse, my enlightened yogi, my colossal pillar of support and my creative genius. You are the love of my life! My best friend. Every breath you take is a gift that I am so blessed to receive. My love for you would explode these pages if I tried to put it into words, so I won't, because I want folks to read this book. This life is our adventure and from your love I spring forth like a lion! Rawr.

Mom and Dad, your love made my little body from scratch, and you tirelessly supported me on my spiritual journey. You fed and clothed me while I was gallivanting through the cosmos. You supported me when I crashed and burned. And still held me up when I was healing my soul. You are remarkable human beings, beyond what I could've wished for. I love you to infinity! Thanks for sharing this life with me, because without you, I wouldn't be the same "me." ;)

Bro, your compassion and kindness are an inspiration. I love you so much. You are courageous and have an incredible soul. I couldn't have imagined a better little brother.

Maharishi Mahesh Yogi, you taught me to devour silence and glimpse God's heart as my own. Your mission in this world was so vast, and I am so humbly thankful to be a part of it. You were infinity in form and you led me to taste that which is formless. Learning your powerful meditation practice (TM) was worth every last transformation. Thank you for making my life truly meaningful by giving me the ability to explore the depths of my soul.

Matthew and Carol, thank you with all my heart for being my guides, my friends, my soul family. Your work as healers in this world is a gift that I am so lucky to receive. You both have taught me so much; I am eternally grateful. You are my dearest friends. I couldn't have done any of this without you.

and finally…

My Sweet God, thank you for manifesting Creation. You make me more whole than I could have ever dreamed.

SPIRITUAL RESOURCES

Transcendental Meditation, founded by Maharishi Mahesh Yogi, is a simple, natural, effortless technique for the promotion of health, creativity, happiness and enlightenment. To learn more, please visit www.TM.org or call 888-LEARN-TM.

The Wholeness School for Sacred Living offers tools and knowledge to empower those on the path to God Awareness. Included are powerful practices and techniques for awakening and breakthrough technologies to allow the human physiology to reach its full potential. To learn more, please visit www.TheWholeness.org/the-wholeness-school or call 888-828-2271.

Matthew Reifslager, founder of The Wholeness and Reifslager Energy Healing, is a spiritual teacher, energy healer, and guide. He provides healing from acute illness and chronic physical and emotional suffering. Matthew also offers support and activations that awaken the full potential of life—both human and divine. To learn more, please visit www.MatthewReifslager.com or call 888-510-1536.

RECOMMENDED READING

Autobiography of a Yogi by Paramahansa Yogananda is a remarkable book written about one man's journey to enlightenment in 20th century India. This insightful account provides inspiration for any seeker on the path to God-realization.

Maharishi Mahesh Yogi on the Bhagavad Gita: A New Translation and Commentary is considered one of the best renditions of this ancient text available. Maharishi beautifully touches on the fundamental life lessons that everyone on earth faces, with profound clarity and grace.

The Power of Now and *A New Earth*, both written by Eckhart Tolle, ask the reader to move beyond the overactive mind into the power of the moment. His books provide a much-needed perspective for seekers awakening in the "spiritual Wild West" that is the 21st century. Eckhart is a true spiritual genius. His work is simultaneously profound and easy to understand.

Love Poems from God: Twelve Sacred Voices from the East and West, translated by Daniel Ladinsky, is a mystic poetry book that offers priceless accounts of saints from Christian, Hindu, and Sufi spiritual traditions. Ladinsky breathes life into the words of these ancient souls and feeds them to the reader in a poetic banquet that is sure to open any heart.

The Wholeness Volume I, by healer and teacher Matthew Reifslager, provides gentle and powerful healings on every page. This book is a lighthouse for any modern day seeker, offering profound and simple techniques to further spiritual growth.

ABOUT THE AUTHOR

L yric Benson Fergusson emerged from almost a decade of study-
ing consciousness and enlightenment to create her debut album
Lyric's Love Light Revolution, co-produced by her father, actor/direc-
tor Robby Benson, and her singer/songwriter mother, Karla DeVito.
The album is a celebration of Lyric's wildly eccentric journey into the
throes of divine love. All of her lyrics were inspired and taken directly
from the poetry she composed over these very unconventional spiri-
tual years.

With a quiver of over 2,000 poems under her belt, Lyric is
now stepping out and sharing a 108 of her intimate favorites
in this transformational book, *French Kissing God: A Journey to
Enlightenment.*

Lyric grew up in Hollywood and is an enthusiastic screenwriter
(she attended NYU Tisch Film School), poet, actress, photographer,
spiritual teacher, and activist. An avid practitioner of Maharishi
Mahesh Yogi's Transcendental Meditation, she graduated Magna
Cum Laude from Maharishi University of Management in 2006 with
a degree in Vedic Science. It was this experience that led Lyric to delve
deep within herself in an exploration of consciousness, fueling her
desire for enlightenment.

Lyric has spent many years as a teacher of The Wholeness, a non-profit organization dedicated to facilitating the full awakening of humanity. She has been deeply transformed and inspired by their breakthrough technologies, which bring each individual's awareness back to the love and truth resonating in all of our hearts.

Lyric is also honored and excited to help kick-start GATE's NextGen, which inspires young artists to change the world. GATE, the Global Alliance for Transformational Entertainment, is a non-profit charitable organization founded in 2009 by John Raatz, Jim Carrey, Eckhart Tolle, and David Langer for artists and interested individuals who acknowledge the vital and expanding roles media and entertainment play in creating our lives, and who aspire to consciously transform those domains for the benefit of all.

Lyric is currently living in Maui, Hawai'i, with her remarkable husband Asher Fergusson, and is deeply grateful for the journey this life has provided.

Additional Contact Information

If you're interested in scheduling Lyric for a speaking engagement please email her at the address below.

Email: Lyric@FrenchKissingGod.com
Website: www.FrenchKissingGod.com
Facebook: www.Facebook.com/FrenchKissingGod
Twitter: www.Twitter.com/FrenchKissinGod

Cover art by www.RosalievandenBos.com
Photography by www.AsherFergusson.com

FRENCH KISSING GOD
P.O. Box 197
Wailuku, HI, 96793, USA

FREE BONUS
MATERIALS

P lease visit www.FrenchKissingGod.com/Gifts to get free instant access to my bonus materials. These include MP3 downloads from my spiritual rock'n'roll album *Lyric's Love Light Revolution* and other free gifts.

Made in United States
Orlando, FL
15 February 2023